Original title:
Laughs from the Lattice

Copyright © 2025 Creative Arts Management OÜ
All rights reserved.

Author: Adeline Fairfax
ISBN HARDBACK: 978-1-80567-356-9
ISBN PAPERBACK: 978-1-80567-655-3

Hilarity on the Hideaway

In a nook where shadows play,
Silly birds sing night and day.
A squirrel spins a wobbly tale,
While grasshoppers hop without fail.

With a grin, the sun peeks through,
Tickling leaves with a golden hue.
Laughter bounces on the breeze,
As giggles dance among the trees.

Bubbly Breezes

Puffed clouds form a playful crowd,
Ticklish winds are bright and loud.
A rainbow arc, a joyful sight,
Spreading cheer with pure delight.

Lemonade spills from giggling jugs,
Farmers dance with their furry hugs.
Funny faces painted bright,
Chasing shadows with pure light.

Carefree Canopies

Underneath a leafy dome,
Butterflies flit, they find their home.
A rabbit hops, a kitten purrs,
An orchestra of joyful blurs.

Sunbeams peek through branches wide,
With party hats, the critters glide.
Each rustle stirs a chortled sound,
In this realm where fun is found.

Jovial Hideouts

Amidst the trees, a secret spot,
Where whispers giggle and laughter's caught.
Swinging vines invite the game,
Each turn and twist, a new acclaim.

A turtle guides a silly race,
While raccoons juggle with such grace.
Here, the world unveils its charm,
In moments where hearts stay warm.

Breezy Banter

A squirrel dressed in shades so bright,
Chased a shadow, oh what a sight!
With each leap, a giggle arose,
Even the flowers swayed, I suppose.

A raccoon with a pie on his head,
Waltzed around where the neighbors tread.
In the moonlight, he took a bow,
Making us laugh, oh how, oh how!

Dappled Joys

The sunbeams danced on a bumblebee,
Tickling petals with glee, you see!
With every buzz, they shared a tease,
A banquet of nectar, a banquet of bees.

A puppy rolled in a patch of grass,
Chasing its tail while the daisies pass.
In the chaos, a wiggle and wag,
And we burst out, our hearts in a rag.

Heartfelt Humor

A cat in a hat tried to sing an old tune,
But it mumbled, like a rather grumpy loon.
With paws in the air, it gave quite a show,
We laughed till we cried, oh such blissful glow!

Two turtles raced, oh what a delight,
One took a nap, the other took flight.
With a shell so sturdy, they made us cheer,
What a spectacle! Let's all grab a beer!

Cackles in the Canes

Behind the reeds, a wild duck quacked,
As a frog with a vest cheekily clacked.
They formed a duet, silly and loud,
Drawing in birds, a curious crowd.

In the tall grass, a jester appeared,
With mischief abound, the laughter steered.
With a wink and a jig, he made merry sound,
The whole glade sparkled, fun all around.

Lively Leans

A squirrel in a tux, on a tree,
Checks his watch and calls for tea.
The birds, they giggle, tweet in delight,
As acorns tumble in the soft twilight.

A raccoon juggles with shiny stones,
While rabbits laugh at his funny tones.
The branches sway with a playful tune,
As shadows dance beneath the moon.

Glee Within the Grid

Sunbeams play peek-a-boo in the park,
A dog rolls over, oh, what a lark!
Kites twist and turn in the warm, blue sky,
While kids chase clouds, giggling, oh my!

The fence posts wiggle, full of surprise,
As butterflies waltz, oh how they rise!
Each step is a dance, every glance a cheer,
In this joyful grid, happiness steers.

Chuckles in the Crevices

A chipmunk peeks from a tiny hole,
With a nut in hand, he finds his role.
Raccoons enter the scene, playful and bold,
Stealing snacks — oh, the stories they told!

Between the stones, mischief thrives,
Every crevice a stage where laughter survives.
Nature's own jesters, in fur and in fluff,
Whispering jokes, just can't get enough!

Whispers of Joyful Ironwork

A twist of metal gleams so bright,
Whispers of joy dance in the light.
In playful shapes, with glee they bend,
Telling secrets, they never end.

A spider spins with flair and pride,
Each web a joke, spun far and wide.
The shadows giggle, stretch and sway,
In iron's embrace, they play all day.

Giggling Through the Grilles

Windows framed with clever style,
Peek through and find a cheeky smile.
The bars, they chatter, jive, and swing,
With every breeze, they start to sing.

Between the grates, a playful tease,
A breeze of laughter, wild with ease.
They rattle softly, join the cheer,
As giggles rise, they linger near.

Chortles in the Garden's Embrace

In blooms and greens, the heart takes flight,
 The garden chuckles, pure delight.
 Each petal sways, with humor there,
  In nature's script, a joyful air.

 A bumblebee hums a silly tune,
  Dancing 'round the sunlit June.
 The flowers nod, with bashful grace,
 Each laugh embraced in gentle space.

Chuckles Beneath the Twisted Vines

Vines entwine in a merry race,
They tickle stars in their embrace.
Fingers of green, with mischief play,
Weaving tales in a vine-fringed way.

The roots below chuckle, deepest sound,
As laughter lifts, it knows no bounds.
In tangled joy, the world unwinds,
A banter shared, where heart aligns.

Glee in the Gazebo

In the shade where shadows dance,
A breeze plays tricks, a happy chance.
Squirrels dart with cheeky glee,
While birds perform in harmony.

Beneath the roof of woven dreams,
Laughter bubbles, or so it seems.
Chasing leaves that whirl and twirl,
Butterflies spin in a joyous swirl.

Friends gather round with silly tales,
As laughter echoes like soft gales.
The cracks in benches hold our cheer,
Each giggle ringing loud and clear.

With lemonade fresh and cookies sweet,
We find joy in each simple treat.
A day like this, so light and bright,
Woven memories in dazzling light.

Radiance of the Ropes

From tree to tree, the ropes will swing,
Inviting all to join and cling.
With every bounce and silly grin,
The day's adventures soon begin.

Up high, the brave will laugh and cheer,
While below, a ticklish fear.
A playful tug and jolly shake,
Who knew the fun that they could make?

Each knot a tale, each swing a song,
We find delight where we belong.
With every twist, we share a shout,
In this bright world, there's no doubt.

Together we sway beneath the sun,
In this merry dance, we are one.
With radiant smiles and spirits free,
In laughter's glow, we find the key.

Cheery Encounters

On a path where neighbors greet,
Every smile feels like a treat.
With funny faces, winks, and grins,
The laughter starts, and joy begins.

A dog arrives with shoes in tow,
Its happy bark, a comic show.
The tree swings low, a playful space,
Where clouds of giggles leave a trace.

With stories spun and jokes unplanned,
We branch out more; we're not just friends.
Crows caw through the leafy shade,
As laughter grows, and worries fade.

Each twist of fate, a fun surprise,
Sparkling warmth in each other's eyes.
Cheer spills forth like a bright parade,
In these encounters, joy is made.

Bustling Vignettes

In bustling lanes where stories bloom,
Quirky moments burst with room.
A hat shop bursting with silly wear,
Giggles echo through the air.

The baker grins with frosting bright,
A pie flies high; oh, what a sight!
With every step, a tale unfolds,
In vibrant hues, the laughter molds.

Children play in puddles deep,
Their joyful shrieks an endless leap.
With ice cream drips and playful shouts,
They weave through life with serendipity routes.

Watch the juggler and his flair,
He drops a ball; the crowd's affair.
In this rich tapestry of glee,
Each moment's magic, wild and free.

Witty Breezes Through the Trellis

A breeze tickles the leaves, so light,
Whispers of jest in the fading light.
Giggling vines twist in playful runs,
Chasing the shadows, the day just begun.

Frisky shadows dance in the sun,
A symphony played, oh what fun!
Jokes wrapped in petals, a vibrant show,
Nature's own humor, just watch it flow.

Laughter peeks from each tiny bud,
Colors collide, a delightful flood.
With every rustle, a punchline's found,
Joy blooms where the laughter's unbound.

A trellis entwined, a jester's stage,
Life's carefree antics, coming of age.
So come take a seat, hear the fun unfold,
Witty breezes whisper, their stories told.

Sunlit Chuckles in Hidden Nooks

In corners where sunlight loves to play,
Gentle giggles chase shadows away.
Curious critters peek through the green,
Hidden laughter flows, a joyful scene.

Sunbeams dance with a mischievous wink,
Bouncing from leaves, making them blink.
Mirrored in puddles, a chuckle remains,
Nature's soft humor in laughter's refrains.

Ticklish petals flutter in breeze,
Whispers of joy beneath the tall trees.
Jests swirl and twirl, a playful embrace,
Every nook reveals a smiling face.

Sunlit corners hide stories untold,
Where joy is unwrapped, bright, and bold.
So pause for a moment, take it all in,
In secretive spaces, let laughter begin.

Playful Spirits in Decorative Patterns

Colors collide in a splendid array,
Each twist and turn leads the heart to play.
Patterns emerge with a wink and a grin,
A parade of joy that draws you in.

Painted petals, a dance on the breeze,
Spirits of mirth, such moments to seize.
Curls and swirls, a jest in each line,
Nature's own laughter, delightful design.

Dancing shadows performed by the light,
Whimsical stories unfurling in flight.
A tapestry woven of giggles and cheer,
In each vibrant corner, joy's drawing near.

Celebrate colors and laughter's embrace,
In these decorative patterns, find your place.
So let your heart giggle, your spirit feel free,
For the playful spirits are waiting, you'll see.

Secrets of Joy in Interlaced Branches

Branches entwine, a clandestine space,
Secrets of joy in a wild embrace.
Laughter's perfume floats in the air,
Tales of delight, spun with such care.

Whispering winds tease the leaves overhead,
Filling the world with the words left unsaid.
In the heart of the grove, find solace and play,
Where joy intertwines in a jubilant sway.

Each knot and twist, a story to tell,
Winding in rhythms, they weave their spell.
Unruly and free, the branches conspire,
Igniting a spark, a joyous fire.

So step out and venture where laughter takes root,
In interlaced branches, let joy be your fruit.
The secrets of gladness await to be found,
In nature's embrace, let your heart know its sound.

Light-hearted Latticework

In gardens bright with blooming cheer,
Tiny critters scurry near.
With antics grand, they dance and play,
Turning mundane into a display.

A breeze whispers through leaves and twines,
Tickling noses, drawing lines.
In shadows cast by frames so fair,
Giggles linger in the air.

The sun peeks through with golden beams,
Chasing after playful dreams.
While squirrels dart and birds take flight,
Each moment bursts with pure delight.

We weave the joys with threads of light,
Embracing laughter, pure and bright.
With every twist and turn that's spun,
Laughter rings as we all have fun.

Serendipitous Snickers

In the corner of the yard, a sight,
A cat attempts a daring flight.
Bouncing back from wooden beams,
Fluffy fails provoke our schemes.

Amidst the winks of glistening eyes,
A puppy stumbles, full of surprise.
With wagging tails and silly sights,
Our hearts are tangled in pure light.

Chasing shadows, up they leap,
The world a canvas, laughter deep.
Sprinkling joy like morning dew,
When mischief dances, friendships brew.

In moments shared, we find our glee,
The simple things set laughter free.
With playful pranks and joyful grins,
Life's best moments always win.

Grins Beneath the Gaze

Beneath the trellis, laughter wakes,
Where friends convene for silly breaks.
With whispered jokes and winks aside,
In nature's warmth, we take our stride.

A dog trots in with muddy paws,
Leaving prints that bring forth applause.
We chuckle as he shakes his head,
Creating rainbows where he treads.

Under the watch of leafy green,
Wit and whimsy weave a scene.
With every jest and playful tease,
The weight of life is light as breeze.

So let us share this merry time,
With giggles that could spark a rhyme.
In joyous moments, bonds we build,
With laughter's brush, our hearts are filled.

Frolics on the Fencing

On wooden rails, the boundless fun,
Where children play and shadows run.
They leap and climb, with voices bright,
Creating a world of pure delight.

The wind it flickers, whispers low,
As giggles carry, up they go.
With every tumble, falls and spins,
The joyful echoes invite grins.

A cat meanders, all aloof,
Observing antics from the roof.
With every pounce, each playful squeal,
The laughter blooms, a vibrant reel.

From dawn's first light to evening's shade,
In fun and frolic, memories made.
So gather, friends, let laughter sway,
In this embrace, we'll dance and play.

Squiggles of Serenity

On a summer's day, skies of blue,
Children dance and play, it's true.
Sidewalk chalk sprawls, colors collide,
Laughter and giggles, joy can't hide.

A cat on a swing, oh what a sight,
Chasing its tail, what pure delight.
With each little pounce and curious meow,
The whole world stops, everyone bows.

Jellybeans tumble, candies take flight,
Silly faces, oh what a sight.
Ice cream cone slides, a playful slip,
Sticky fingers, laughter won't quit.

In the garden, flowers wiggle and sway,
Bees in their suits dance away.
With nature's antics, joy feels complete,
In this melody, life feels sweet.

The Eloquent Eaves

Whispers of laughter, secrets unfold,
Behind every door, stories are told.
Eavesdropping giggles, fun in the air,
A parade of mishaps, none can compare.

A baker drops pies, filling in flight,
The cat steals a crust, oh what a sight!
Grandma's lost glasses, on top of her head,
A humorous twist, nothing to dread.

Splatters of paint, a colorful mess,
Sprinkles of joy, who could guess?
Chairs dance around, pretending to prance,
In this quiet room, they all take a chance.

Against the window, raindrops tap-tap,
A rhythmic story, a comical map.
The world outside, silly creatures in line,
With each little giggle, the sun starts to shine.

Laughing Lightly

Ticklish winds across the green fields,
Waving goodbye, as nature yields.
Frogs in the pond put on a show,
Jumping and croaking, go with the flow.

Butterflies flutter with mischievous flair,
Chasing each other, dancing in air.
A squirrel dons nuts like a fashionista,
Strutting its stuff, oh what a fiesta!

A tumble of leaves in a gusty embrace,
They spin 'round and 'round, a wild chase.
Laughter erupts from the trees and the brook,
Nature's own tales, you simply can't book.

As twilight approaches, stars start to peek,
With whispers of joy, the night starts to speak.
A chorus of giggles floats through the dusk,
In this merry moment, life's golden musk.

Grinning Through the Gaps

In the cracks of the pavement, a sprout takes a stand,
Determined, it reaches, bending with the land.
A smile from the sun, as bright as can be,
Bringing warmth and laughs, carefree and free.

Chickens in sunglasses scratching for crumbs,
Strutting their stuff, as if mating for drums.
A quirky parade on the farm draws near,
With clucks and with crows, it's hard not to cheer.

An old dog on a skateboard, cruising along,
Wagging its tail to the upbeat song.
Puddles of joy, reflections of glee,
Radiate laughter, wild and carefree.

So when life gets tough and joy's hard to find,
Look for the silly, the easy, the kind.
For grinning through gaps shows laughter can spread,
In the simplest moments, happiness bred.

Witty Whispers

In a garden filled with glee,
The flowers start to giggle free.
A breeze tells jokes, a rustle sweet,
As petals dance on light, they meet.

Silly ants march in a line,
Each step a cha-cha, how divine!
With tiny hats and dainty shoes,
They groove to tunes that chase the blues.

A squirrel twerks upon a branch,
With acorn bling, he takes a chance.
While butterflies applaud his flair,
The sun can't help but join the air.

Beneath the moon, the shadows play,
They swap their secrets, night and day.
In whispers soft, the starlight beams,
A symphony of giggling dreams.

The Art of Amusement

A painting made of chuckle hues,
On canvas bright with joyful views.
The brush of laughter strokes the night,
Creating smiles that feel so light.

Clowns in colors, wild and bold,
With juggling tricks and tales retold.
They tumble down, yet rise again,
In every fall, a joyful gain.

A parrot mimics every word,
With wit so sharp, it seems absurd.
It cracks a joke that makes hearts soar,
The merriment forevermore.

In every corner, glee unfolds,
With magic tricks and tales of old.
The canvas thick with joy and grace,
In this gallery, we find our place.

Carousels of Cheer

Round and round the ponies spin,
With glitter eyes that laugh and grin.
A parade of joy on every sway,
Bright ribbons whip the clouds away.

The music plays, a merry tune,
While bunnies hop beneath the moon.
They bounce along with gleeful shouts,
In circles wide, they dance about.

A cotton candy storm arrives,
With sugary clouds that tickle lives.
As kids all cheer, the laughter flows,
Each bite a giggle, sweetness grows.

The carousel, a whirl of fun,
With painted dreams, it's never done.
In joy's embrace, we all unite,
For in this world, the mood is right.

Echoes of Enchantment

Through the woods where echoes play,
The trees have jokes they like to sway.
With every breeze a chuckle flows,
The forest laughs where magic grows.

The rabbits tell a tale so grand,
Of dancing feet and funny bands.
With every hop, a joke is made,
In leafy shades, the laughter's laid.

The brook tells tales with bubbling sound,
It sparkles bright, joy all around.
Each ripple sings a playful rhyme,
A serenade of fun, sublime.

In twilight's glow, the fireflies wink,
As twilight brings a playful link.
The night unfolds its charming spell,
In echoes warm, we laugh and dwell.

Snickers from the Leafy Canopy

Breezes tickle branches high,
Squirrels chatter as they fly.
Leaves whisper tales of the day,
Nature giggles in a playful way.

Sunlight dances on the ground,
Jokes in shadows can be found.
A flower blooms with a cheeky smirk,
While worms do their little quirk.

Birds break into a silly song,
Their notes flutter, like a throng.
In the canopy, laughter swells,
Echoes of all nature's tales.

Amidst the trees where fun aligns,
Joy blooms in zigzag lines.
A breeze carries soft delight,
In leafy realms, all feels just right.

Smiles Through the Screen of Time

Glimmers of joy in pixel frames,
A world of laughter, no two the same.
Time dances on its digital feet,
Funny messages, oh what a treat!

Threads of giggles, a meme parade,
Cackles and chuckles that never fade.
In every swipe, a jest unfolds,
Stories of humor, brightly told.

The glow of the screen, a beacon bright,
Waves of happiness take flight.
In every picture, joy resides,
Fueling laughter that never hides.

Together we share, we jest and cheer,
Through time and space, the fun is near.
With each new post, we find our way,
In the garden of smiles, we play.

Mirthful Moments in the Arboretum

Blossoms bobbing in a breeze,
With playful spirits, they tease.
Sunbeams play in every nook,
While a busy bee steals a look.

Laughter rings from every tree,
Rooted in glee, they seem so free.
A chipmunk grins, chestnut in paw,
Turning sights into pure awe.

Petals waltz with the wind's sweet song,
In this world, we all belong.
Moments weave in bright tapestry,
A twist of mirth in nature's spree.

In the garden where happiness grows,
Every creature knows how it flows.
In playful ways, we laugh and cheer,
Creating memories that draw us near.

The Delight of Unexpected Turns

Life's path twists in hilarious ways,
Around each corner, a joke that stays.
With every turn, surprises bloom,
Filling hearts with joyful room.

Stumbling upon a puddled grin,
Every blunder feels like a win.
With laughter trailing behind our feet,
Navigating life, a fun retreat.

Oh, what joy that life can bring,
When we learn to dance and sing.
Each misstep a chance to jest,
Finding the fun in every quest.

So here's to the turns we embrace,
Each laughter shared, a warm embrace.
In the journey, we all will find,
Delights that tickle the heart and mind.

Sprightly Serenades

Under the sun, a dance begins,
Birds chirp joy, their playful spins.
A squirrel hops on a crowded fence,
Chasing shadows, such great suspense.

Children's giggles fill the air,
Tiny feet, without a care.
A kite swirls, caught in the breeze,
Painting the sky with playful ease.

Bubbles in the Blossoms

In a garden where colors gleam,
Bubbles float like a daydream.
Petals giggle, swaying by,
Tickled by the whispers of July.

A ladybug wears a tiny hat,
Waddles by, just like that!
With every pop, a laugh escapes,
Creating tales in flower shapes.

Mirth Among the Maple

Maple leaves dance in delight,
Whirling colors, a joyful sight.
Acorns tumble, a clumsy show,
Nature's chuckles, off they go.

The breeze plays tricks on the trees,
Rustling laughter, easy to tease.
A raccoon peeks from its cozy nook,
Stealing snacks with a playful look.

The Playful Pavilion

Under the arch where shadows play,
Laughter echoes, come what may.
Children chase with squeals so bright,
Turning day into pure delight.

A jester leaps and takes a bow,
Tickling fancies, here and now.
Balloons dance with the evening stars,
Sharing secrets from near and far.

Giggling with the Grape Vines

In the vineyard where the sun beams,
Grapes hang low, bursting at the seams.
A squirrel dances, tails a-twirl,
Chasing shadows in a whimsical swirl.

Wobbling barrels roll down the lane,
They bounce with joy, not a hint of pain.
The breeze carries whispers, sweet and spry,
As laughter flutters like birds in the sky.

Tiny twigs play peek-a-boo,
While blossoms giggle, fresh with dew.
Underneath the green canopy, they prance,
In a vineyard ballet, oh what a chance!

Sunset paints the fruit all aglow,
As echoes ripple, soft and slow.
The grapes chuckle, a jolly jest,
In this vineyard, life's simply the best!

Radiant Reflections

Mirror lakes glisten, bright and clear,
With a hint of mischief, they draw us near.
Ripples giggle, tickled by the breeze,
As turtles laugh beneath the trees.

The sun plays tag with shadows' dance,
In this vibrant realm of happenstance.
Each startled fish leaps with glee,
Creating splashes, wild and free.

The setting sun throws colors bold,
Golden hues with a story to be told.
As fireflies twirl in glowing bands,
Magic unfolds, across the lands.

In this realm where joy reflects,
Every moment brightly connects.
Nature's canvas, painted with cheer,
Whispers of laughter, oh so near!

Uplifting Echoes

High on the hills where the wildflowers sway,
Echoes of giggles drift far away.
A butterfly flutters, a playful sight,
Chasing its friends as they take flight.

The clouds puff up, like popcorn, so light,
Transforming the day into pure delight.
Each breeze carries whispers, soft and low,
As the world around us begins to glow.

Crisp autumn leaves dance in the air,
Rustling secrets of laughter to share.
Bouncing off stones, the giggles ring clear,
Nature rejoices, spreading good cheer.

In this bright haven, we leap and play,
Moments of joy, forever to stay.
With every echo, our spirits soar high,
Lifting our hearts, in this colorful sky!

Merry Groves

In the heart of the woods, laughter resounds,
With shadows and sunshine, joy abounds.
Squirrels chatter, their antics on show,
As chipmunks join in, putting on a show.

Boughs sway with music, a whimsical tune,
As flowers giggle 'neath the glowing moon.
The owls hoot softly, sharing a jest,
While crickets rejoice, in this nature's fest.

Breezes tickle the leaves, a playful tease,
Echoes of fun float from tree to tree.
Each path we wander, a new tale spun,
In these merry groves, we become one.

As day turns to night, the laughter remains,
A symphony sweet, where joy never wanes.
In the heart of the woods, magic unravels,
In merry groves, where the spirit travels!

Bliss in the Bower

Where whispers weave in leafy dreams,
The sun spills gold in playful beams.
A squirrel dances, tails a-flight,
In joy's embrace, all feels just right.

The flowers nod, their colors bright,
While butterflies take off in flight.
The laughter echoes, pure and clear,
Inviting all who wander near.

A picnic spread with treats galore,
Sandwiches stacked, tumbling to the floor!
Juice spills, and giggles fill the air,
In this haven, none a single care.

So here we chuckle, side by side,
Amidst the blooms, our hearts abide.
Each moment's burst, a sweet delight,
In nature's arms, everything feels right.

Grinning with the Greens

In the garden, fun does sprout,
With silly weeds that dance about.
The peas all giggle, plump and proud,
While carrots peek above the crowd.

Lettuce leaves with laughter sway,
In sunshine's warmth they like to play.
Tomatoes blush, a rosy hue,
With grapevines grinning just for you.

A rabbit hops, he takes a bow,
"A feast awaits, come join us now!"
As bugs and blooms unite in cheer,
Within this patch, we shed a tear.

So raise a toast with fruits and greens,
To all the joy that nature means.
With every chuckle, let's inspire,
A heart that dances, never tires.

Jesting in the Juxtaposition

In mismatched socks, we start the day,
A case of giggles, come what may.
With buttons bold and colors bright,
Our outfits clash in pure delight.

The cat, now perched upon the chair,
Wears a crown of flowers, what a flair!
He tosses glances, half amused,
As noisy ants have him confused.

A teapot grins, its spout adorned,
With steaming tea, the table's sworn.
Each cup a secret, laughter spills,
As stories twist with funny thrills.

So here we sit, misfits in style,
With chuckles and joy, let's stay awhile.
For in this blend of oddity,
We find our hearts in unity.

Exuberance in the Edges

At the fringe of fields, the fray begins,
Where laughter tumbles, and joy wins.
The daisies sway with playful grace,
A runaway breeze makes smiles race.

In corners crowded, stories unfold,
With whispers soft, yet laughter bold.
A puppy prances, chasing his tail,
While shadows dance, and spirits sail.

The sun dips low, igniting the skies,
As stars blink slowly, with winking eyes.
Each chuckle echoes through the night,
In edge's embrace, the world feels right.

So gather close, let merriment flow,
In the laughter where wildflowers grow.
For here we bask in the joy we find,
In every giggle, we're intertwined.

Radiant Riddles in the Greenery

Among the leaves, a secret brews,
Where whispers tickle morning dew.
A gnome giggles, hat askew,
And dancing fairies sing their blues.

A rabbit hops with playful grace,
Chasing shadows, a wild chase.
In sunlight's glow, a smiling face,
The garden plays its funny ace.

Each flower bows with cheeky flair,
As bees buzz by without a care.
In nature's jest, we find our share,
Where every breeze is light and rare.

With every twist, a tale unfolds,
In vibrant hues, the laughter molds.
The greenery, with secrets told,
In this bright world, we're never old.

The Lightness of Framed Memories

In frames of wood, the tales reside,
Of picnic ants that love to slide.
Each photo sparks a grin inside,
As laughter chases fears aside.

A squirrel peeks from yonder tree,
With acorns nestled comfortably.
Each snapshot giggles, full of glee,
Capturing life, capriciously.

In cobwebbed corners, dust bunnies dance,
Taking each moment, creating a chance.
With chuckles flowing, as we prance,
These light reflections make us glance.

Then comes the sunset, warm and bright,
With memories framed in gentle light.
Each joyful moment takes its flight,
In laughter's glow, everything feels right.

Elation in the Understory

Beneath the trees, where shadows play,
A rabbit's foot leads the fray.
With twitching nose, he hops away,
In leafy lanes, it's child's play.

A chattering bird sings silly songs,
As worms wiggle to dance along.
In this green world where nothing's wrong,
Laughter rings, vibrant and strong.

The mushrooms boast their polka dots,
As ants engage in funny plots.
In nature's realms, with all its quirks,
We find the joy that always lurks.

With every step, new giggles bloom,
In sunlight's grace, no hint of gloom.
In every patch, the air's a room,
Where happiness finds its happy tune.

Humorous Ways of the Garden Path

On winding trails where daisies poke,
A mischievous fox shares a joke.
With floppy ears and clever stroke,
Each pebble laughs beneath a cloak.

The wayward paths twist and twine,
Where turtles take their time, divine.
With every turn, a punchline's shine,
The garden's comedy is truly fine.

As wildflowers sway, a mystery brews,
Where bees wobble, wearing hues.
In this land of whimsical views,
Every curlicue brings happy news.

So come and wander, don't be shy,
In this patch, giggles freely fly.
With playful spirits soaring high,
We'll chuckle out beneath the sky.

Whims of Wind Through Woven Frames

In the garden, breezes play,
Twisting leaves in light ballet.
A giggle here, a laugh out loud,
Nature's jest, a joyous crowd.

Branches dance with swaying tune,
Teasing sunlight, bright as noon.
The shadows leap and weave about,
In this spectacle, joy's no doubt.

Petals flutter, chuckles rise,
Caught mid-air, a sweet surprise.
Fluttering wings and whispers tease,
Woven frames, delightful breeze.

Laughter mingles in the air,
Echoes of a playful dare.
Nature's humor brings a cheer,
Crafted joys, a world sincere.

Chuckling Canopies Above

High above, the leaves conspire,
Winking at the sun's desire.
Clouds tiptoe on a gentle breeze,
Hiding smiles among the trees.

Each rustle sings a secret song,
A jolly tune where all belong.
Branches sway, a playful dance,
Encouraging a light-filled trance.

Underneath, the grass joins in,
A carpet bright, where laughs begin.
Dancing shadows flit and tease,
Removing worries with such ease.

Nature's laughter fills the air,
Creating moments free from care.
Through our joy, the world we weave,
In chuckling canopies, we believe.

The Artistry of Amused Greenery

In every leaf, a grin is found,
As breezes carry laughter 'round.
Colors burst in dazzling displays,
Tickling senses through sunny rays.

Twisting vines in playful schemes,
Fill the air with merry dreams.
Every petal has a jest,
In this landscape, smiles invest.

Bushes giggle, shrubs embrace,
In this lively, vibrant space.
Whispers weave through every nook,
Crafting joy, a quirky book.

Artistry in every shade,
In nature's game, we're all arrayed.
We dance along in verdant glee,
Bound by laughter, wild and free.

Jocular Trails in the Arboreal Maze

Through the woods, a path unfolds,
Where each twist a tale retolds.
The branches wave, welcoming fun,
As shadows play beneath the sun.

A squirrel hops, a bird will tease,
Nature's jesters aim to please.
With every turn, a surprise waits,
In the maze of laughing fates.

Dappled light, a playful glow,
Follow the giggles, up and low.
Footsteps echo, a joyous squeal,
In this bouncy tapestry, we feel.

Jocular sights that make hearts sing,
In lively woods, let laughter spring.
Together here, we've found our way,
In arboreal delights, we sway.

Mirth Amidst the Woven Shadows

Beneath the trellis, whispers play,
A jester's grin at the end of day.
With shadows dancing, twirls of light,
Each chuckle hides a playful bite.

The sunbeams chase the bugs that zoom,
While old vines tease the flowers in bloom.
A squirrel pauses, struck with glee,
As blooms of laughter set him free.

In corners where the ivy creeps,
They share their secrets, not a peep.
Each leaf a witness, every twist,
To tales of joy that none dare miss.

From woven strands of nature's art,
Spring's jests take root, a joyful start.
A tapestry of mirth unfurls,
Through woven shadows, laughter swirls.

Grins Among the Wooden Slats

Among the posts, the mischief brews,
With subtle jests and playful cues.
The wind it giggles through the cracks,
As sunlight radiates, no lacks.

The fence post wobbles, what a sight!
As critters skitter left and right.
Each wooden slat holds stories tight,
Of funny moments and pure delight.

When evening settles, loons will croon,
While fireflies flicker, a tiny boon.
In moonlit frames, the mischief hides,
With whispers soft, where laughter glides.

Among the wooden slats of joy,
The world transforms with every ploy.
With smiles contagious, nature sings,
And every heart takes flight on wings.

The Humor of Twisted Branches

Beneath the branches, tangled and gnarled,
A humor blooms, untamed and charred.
The owls exchange their quirky looks,
While whispers roam through nature's books.

The dance of leaves in warm sunlight,
Reveals a game, a playful sight.
A gentle breeze with teasing flair,
Plays tricks on all who wander near.

Twists and turns hold laughter's glee,
A squirrel in acorn sabotage spree.
The branches chuckle, twist and sway,
While shadows join the mischief's play.

With every crinkle, every bend,
A story waits around each end.
The humor thrives in wooded stretches,
Where nature weaves her bright sketches.

Jests in the Frame of Nature

In nature's frame, the jests collide,
With blossoms laughing side by side.
The brook hums softly, jokes to tell,
As pebbles giggle, casting a spell.

The daisies chatter, bows they take,
While butterflies play at hide and seek.
Each breeze that ruffles the fragrant bloom,
Adds giggles to the garden's room.

Through tangled weeds and vibrant hues,
Hilarity springs from morning's dews.
The humor flows like nectar sweet,
As nature shares its rhythmic beat.

In frames crafted by sun and shade,
The world unfolds, and joy is laid.
With every rustle, a plot is spun,
In nature's jest, we find our fun.

Whimsical Twists

In the garden where shadows play,
A rabbit wears glasses, bright and gay.
He jogs in circles, a site quite rare,
While a snail cheers him on from a chair.

The sun laughs loud, dipping low in glee,
As squirrels juggle acorns by a tree.
A ladybug rolls, spins on her back,
While grasshoppers dance, keeping no track.

Mirthful Moments

Bubbles float by on a gentle breeze,
As children chase them with giggles and wheezes.
A kite gets stuck in the neighbor's tree,
And the cat looks on with a fit of glee.

The ice cream man slips, spills the delight,
As sprinkles rain down in a colorful flight.
A mouse in a cap steals a piece of cheese,
While onlookers chuckle, their hearts at ease.

Revelry in the Retreat

A pond reflects smiles of frogs in a choir,
Who croak out their tunes by a shimmering fire.
The ducks waddle by, in a comical race,
Splashing in puddles with joy on their face.

Mischief unfolds as a child tells a joke,
While shadows dance lively, the air full of smoke.
Laughter erupts as a turtle turns fast,
In a comedic feat, he wins at the last.

Sprightly Connections

A bumblebee hums through petals of glee,
While whispers of secrets float up from the tree.
A butterfly winks, flutters on by,
Chasing the giggles that soar to the sky.

Friends on the porch with lemonade cups
Share tales of mischief, and life's silly ups.
As evening descends, the stars start to shine,
They reminisce laughter, sweet moments divine.

Mirth in the Mesh

In a garden where shadows play,
Giggles twirl and sway,
A cat on a ledge with a cheeky grin,
Chasing leaves that dance in the wind.

Bubbles rise like secrets shared,
Sunbeams winking, no one is scared,
A gnome with a hat, too big for his head,
Winks at the blooms as they dance in red.

Little frogs leap, making a scene,
In puddles they splash, feeling quite keen,
The daisies whisper their silly dreams,
As daisies seem to burst with gleams.

Under vines where the stories twist,
Laughter bounces, can't be missed,
With tickling breezes that cheerfully roam,
The mesh of the garden feels like home.

Delightful Shadows

Shadows prance on the garden floor,
With whispers soft, like tales of yore,
A squirrel with acorns, so round and bright,
Mocks the sun in a playful fight.

Beneath the trellis, a rabbit hops,
Spinning and twirling, it surely stops,
To nibble a flower, just for a taste,
Paws tapping joyfully, no drop to waste.

The wind tells jokes through branches low,
Each fluttering leaf sings 'go, go, go!'
A ladybug chuckles, her dots align,
As butterflies dream of fancy design.

In corners hidden, petals unfold,
With giggles of color, so bright and bold,
An artist's palette, where memories cling,
In delightful shadows, life's funny spring.

Riddles Among the Rungs

In a trellis of truths, riddles reside,
Twisting and turning, where secrets hide,
A parrot squawking with tales galore,
Leaves rustle softly, always wanting more.

Climbing high makes the whispers grow,
Where laughter tumbles, like a bright rainbow,
A hedgehog jests, with a laugh so wide,
While ants on a mission take joy in the ride.

The sun, with a grin, peeks through the vines,
Casting pranks in zigzag lines,
"I found a treasure," a grasshopper claims,
As playful winds weave silly games.

Among the rungs, a clever surprise,
With giggles and fun, they dance and rise,
Life's a puzzle, a riddle to spin,
In nature's embrace, we all wear a grin.

Jests in the Climbing Greens

Through the climbing greens, jests take flight,
A chorus of colors, joyful delight,
A dragonfly teases the evening glow,
As fireflies wink, putting on a show.

Frogs play hopscotch on lily pads wide,
Counting the stars, the moon as their guide,
While daisies gossip, in whispers so sweet,
Beneath the green veil, where mischief meets.

A turtle in glasses, so wise and so slow,
Listens to stories of where the wind blows,
Each petal a tale, a laugh in the breeze,
Nature's own humor, aiming to please.

In fun-filled greens, the world feels right,
Dancing the night away, such pure delight,
With laughter entwined in each rustling leaf,
Life's light-hearted moments bring joy, like a thief.

Tittering at Twilight

As shadows creep and dance around,
The world is wrapped in a giggle sound.
The moon winks down, a cheeky sight,
As stars begin their twinkling flight.

With flowers swaying, in breezy play,
They whisper secrets of the day.
A squirrel leaps, a playful grin,
And tosses acorns with a spin.

The crickets chirp a jolly tune,
While night unfolds beneath the moon.
A soft chuckle from the trees,
The nightingale sings with such ease.

In twilight's glow, such whimsy flows,
Where laughter thrives and wonder grows.
Each moment tickles, joy's delight,
In this sweet hour, all feels just right.

Cheerful Patterns of Nature

In the garden's burst of color bright,
Bees hum their jokes, what a funny sight.
Petals flutter, a fashion show,
As butterflies steal the splendid glow.

The sun peeks out, a teasing flair,
Tickling daisies swaying with care.
Each rustle whispers tales of glee,
Nature's laughter, wild and free.

A windy breeze joins in the fun,
Spinning leaves like a playful run.
The pond reflects ripples of cheer,
A chorus of giggles fills the sphere.

Bright blooms nod with jovial grace,
Inviting all to join the race.
In cheerful patterns, smiles align,
Nature's joy is truly divine.

Humor in the Hedge

In the hedgerow's tangled embrace,
A hedgehog hides, a playful face.
Spiny jokes tucked all around,
With every shuffle, laughter found.

The bunnies hop with tiny leaps,
Chasing shadows, where mischief creeps.
Each bush a stage for antics bold,
As secret stories are gently told.

A butterfly lands on a twig,
Doing a dance—oh, look at him jig!
While robins chirp, a comic play,
Filling the air with joy every day.

In this patch where giggles grow,
The hedges hum with humor's flow.
Nature's wit, a playful edge,
Within the joy of the humble hedge.

Amusements in the Alcove

In a quiet nook, where daydreams meet,
Laughter bubbles, oh what a treat!
With cushions piled, a cozy scene,
Where whimsy floats like a silver sheen.

The knick-knacks wink from their place,
Each one adorned with a cheeky face.
A gnome with glee waves a tiny hand,
As secrets flicker in this sweet land.

Sunlight dances on painted walls,
While echoing joy in musical calls.
The moments shared, like bubbles rise,
In playful thoughts that never die.

In this alcove, where all can dare,
To let their smiles fill the air.
With heart and humor woven tight,
This sacred space feels just right.

Whimsy in the Weave

Threads of giggles dance and play,
Woven tales in bright array.
A tapestry of silly cliques,
Knots of joy and cheeky tricks.

Each fiber a chuckle, light and free,
Stitched with whimsy, just for me.
Patterns swirl in cheeky jest,
In this weave, we find our best.

Spools of laughter roll about,
Colors bright, there's never doubt.
Patches here, some fluff, some fun,
In this quilt, we all are one.

Snaps and pops like popcorn dreams,
Crafted hooks and heartfelt themes.
With each tug, a giggle glows,
In the weave, a joy that flows.

Playful Perches

Birds of laughter find their space,
Swaying softly, keeping pace.
Branches, swaying, twist and shout,
In their world, there's never doubt.

Perched on limbs of comic grace,
Chasing shadows in the race.
Jokes like seeds in breezy flight,
Sprinkle smiles, day and night.

Chirps and flutters, laughter flies,
In the air, the humor lies.
A twist, a turn, and then a dive,
In this caper, we all thrive.

Sprinkling giggles through the trees,
Whispers tickle with the breeze.
On playful perches, joy cascades,
In every branch, a laughter parades.

Banter by the Blossoms

Petals flutter, whimsies bloom,
In the garden, dispelling gloom.
Banter swirling in the air,
Nature's chatter, light and fair.

Bees with chuckles zip and zoom,
While flowers swing, dispelling doom.
A dance of colors, bright and bold,
Stories shared, as laughter unfolds.

Giggling grass and cheeky sun,
In this patch, we all have fun.
With every sway, a jest is spun,
In the blossoms, joy's begun.

Flutter by, and join the cheer,
Nature's humor lingers near.
Banter flows like gentle streams,
In this space, we live our dreams.

Jestful Intertwining

Threads of mirth begin to twist,
In this fabric, nothing missed.
Each stitch a smile, every loop,
Crafts a chorus, joyful group.

Jestful tales looped in a row,
Whimsies dance in playful flow.
Kinks and curls in every strand,
Laughter's touch, a guiding hand.

Woven moments, bright and spry,
Wrap us up, as minutes fly.
A tapestry of joy to see,
In this mix, we're wild and free.

Intertwining hearts and minds,
In this canvas, joy unwinds.
Colors splash, and glee is spun,
With each laugh, we come undone.

Glee Where Nature Meets Craft

In quirky patterns leaves align,
A dance of branches, oh how they twine!
Frogs in hats leap with delight,
While squirrels plan their next wild flight.

The sun teases the shadows long,
As laughter weaves its merry song.
A quilt of blooms, so bright and bold,
In nature's arms, the joy unfolds.

Wanderlust of the Whimsical Weave

Winds that play with kites on strings,
Spinning tales of playful flings.
Butterflies dance on breezy flights,
Chasing giggles into the nights.

Baskets filled with dreams untold,
Where mischief and magic unfold.
Every thread a story bright,
In the tapestry of pure delight.

Serenades of the Silken Vines

Vines twist like whispers in the air,
Swaying softly without a care.
Giggling blossoms join the tune,
Under the gaze of the laughing moon.

A banquet set on a garden stage,
With jesters wearing leaf and sage.
Nature's circus, wild and free,
Welcoming all to its jubilee.

Mischief Behind the Rustic Battens

Behind the slats where shadows play,
A band of critters frolic and sway.
Rabbits giggle as they hide,
In this charming, playful ride.

With every creak, a secret shared,
Of playful pranks and dreams declared.
Amidst the wood, a tale unfolds,
Of joys that even time upholds.

Playful Patterns

Twirling shadows dance in glee,
Patterns weave a jolly spree.
Each stitch hums a clownish tune,
Underneath the smiling moon.

Colors clash in merry fights,
Knots of mirth in sunny lights.
Giggles bounce from tangled threads,
While playful spirits make their beds.

Laughter spills from woven seams,
Crafting joy in silly dreams.
Swaying fun in breezy cheer,
Whispers of delight draw near.

With every twist, the chuckles rise,
A whimsical parade in guise.
Patterns tease with feathery fun,
A merry game for everyone.

Joy in the Twine

Tangled tales in fibers spun,
Woven stories never done.
Each loop scripts a quirky jest,
Laughter echoes, never rests.

Twine entangles hearts and minds,
In the laughter, joy unwinds.
With every tug, a chuckle springs,
As mischief dances, playtime sings.

Bright threads teasing, never shy,
As giggles bounce and spirits fly.
In the twist, a wink is tossed,
A smile forged, no moment lost.

Winding up the sunny days,
Crafting cheer in crafty ways.
Joyfully wrapped in playful rhyme,
Life's best moments, caught in twine.

Cheeky Corners

Cornered smiles peek and peek,
With every glance, a giggle's sneak.
Mischief lurking just behind,
Cheeky grins, one of a kind.

In the crevices, laughs abound,
Hidden joy in every sound.
Tight spaces where the jokes collide,
Laughter dances, hearts unwind.

Each angle sharp, each jest delight,
In the corners, day turns bright.
Whispers exchanged, in fun's embrace,
Every turn holds a smiling face.

Cheeky corners tease the day,
In their grip, we laugh and play.
A surprise round every bend,
In silly joy, we all transcend.

Jests of the Leaves

Leaves flutter in a cheeky breeze,
Winking at the world with ease.
Rustling whispers, jokes they share,
Tickling the branches, light as air.

With every rustle, laughter flows,
Nature's giggles, everyone knows.
Leaves rejoice in playful dance,
Every sway a light-hearted chance.

Sunlight filters through their play,
Creating shadows that laugh and sway.
A symphony of cheerful sounds,
Joyful antics in leafy bounds.

In laughter's grip, they drop and twirl,
Creating capers, a whirling whirl.
Jests of the leaves, a merry cheer,
In the forest, smiles appear.

Bright Echoes in the Woodwork

In the corners where shadows play,
A squirrel juggles acorns all day.
They tumble and bounce, a nutty parade,
As laughter hides in wood's charade.

A wise old owl with spectacles round,
Spouts puns that leave everyone sound.
The trees nod along to the quirky tale,
As giggles swirl like a soft veil.

A chipmunk prances, all filled with glee,
Telling jokes to the buzzing bee.
They chatter and chirp, each punchline fits,
In this realm where humor never quits.

The wooden beams creak with soft delight,
As shadows dance in playful light.
In bright echoes that ring with cheer,
The magic of mirth is always near.

Whimsy Under the Canopied Arch

Beneath the branches, a jester trips,
Swapping his hat for a pair of lips.
Bubbles of laughter float on the breeze,
As petals spin down from the trees.

A turtle in shades slides past with flair,
Claiming the crown of the fairest hair.
With a wink and a smile, he tells a joke,
As the nearby flowers begin to soak.

A pair of frogs commence a duet,
Their croaks and tocks are a comic set.
With each high leap, the crowd erupts,
As nature's stage has the joy corrupt.

The twilight hues of a giggling sky,
Shine on the whimsy that's dancing by.
A chorus of chuckles fills the air,
In this haven, no one has a care.

Whispers of the Wicker

In the gentle weave of the old wicker chair,
A spider spins webs, but forgets to beware.
He gets tangled in threads of his own design,
As giggles escape from the wicker vine.

A quirky old cat dons a jaunty scarf,
With purrs that are sweet, and no hint of a barf.
He teases the shadows, giving them names,
As laughter erupts in delightful games.

A mouse with a mustache dances with flair,
Waltzing with toasters, a sight quite rare.
With twirls and with spins, the fun never ceases,
In this space where humor releases.

Whispers of joy weave through the night,
Wicker chairs sway under the light.
In this cozy nook where laughter's alive,
The spirit of playfulness always will thrive.

Chortles in the Arbor

In the arbor bright where the sunlight streams,
A rabbit giggles, lost in its dreams.
With carrots in hand, it spins and twirls,
Sharing its chuckles with daisies and pearls.

A parrot perched high shares tales of old,
With a cackle that's bright, and a heart of gold.
He squawks out punchlines that tickle the air,
As folks stop to chuckle, forgetting their care.

The breeze carries whispers of sheer delight,
As flowers sway gently, a colorful sight.
With each sunny moment, the fun multiplies,
Under the canopy, laughter will rise.

In the embrace of the green, let's all rejoice,
For chortles and giggles blend with our voice.
In this haven of charm, where the sun always beams,
We gather in joy, wrapped in whimsy's dreams.

Giggles through the Trellis

A squirrel in a hat, quite absurd,
Dancing on branches, a lively bird.
He trips on a twig, does a pirouette,
Everyone watches, but not one regret.

The flowers all blush, they can't take the tease,
As butterflies giggle, riding the breeze.
A rabbit in boots hops with great flair,
Stomping on daisies without a care.

A jester frog croaks a mischievous tune,
Under the light of a giggling moon.
His crown made of leaves, he takes a bow,
While crickets applaud with their tiny wow.

Beneath the old arch where the vines intertwine,
All creatures gather, sipping on brine.
With every soft chuckle, the air feels so bright,
At twilight, they frolic, a marvelous sight.

Smiles among the Vines

Twisting and turning, the grapes hang with glee,
While bunnies are munching on sweet clover tea.
A hedgehog in sunhat, so jolly and round,
Makes friends with a raccoon who tumbles around.

The vines giggle softly as shadows diverge,
As lizards wear ties to their late-afternoon purge.
A snail in a hurry, he glides with a grin,
Chasing after the laughter, his race to begin.

Bumblebees buzzing in rhythm with cheer,
Tickle the blossoms that bloom far and near.
With each joyful hum, a melody plays,
Creating a symphony just for their days.

A hammock of greenery swings in the breeze,
Encasing the giggles beneath the tall trees.
With each little sparkle, the sunlight ignites,
As smiles dance freely in whimsical flights.

Chuckles in the Canopy

High up in the branches, a parrot recites,
Tales of adventures on colorful flights.
The monkeys all gather to hear him boast,
While swinging and laughing, they toast to their toast.

A caterpillar wiggles, all dressed in fine threads,
Telling of journeys while swaying his heads.
The branches all sway as if joining in,
With chortles and chuckles that spread like a win.

A raccoon with a mask shares his latest prank,
As owls blink their eyes, giving him thanks.
The sunbeams forget to escape from their post,
Snagging on follies that lead to a host.

At dusk, they all yawn, yet laughter still flows,
Chasing the twilight, where silliness grows.
In the canopy's heart, the merriment thrives,
With moments like these, how joyfully lives.

Joys of the Garden Path

Along the garden path, laughter appears,
As hedgehogs engage in a game of pinball spheres.
Each bounce, each giggle, a fragrant delight,
With daisies all swaying in a playful flight.

The mushrooms are chuckling, they wobble and shake,
While frogs tell their stories of epic mistake.
A snail doing summersaults, quite out of line,
Pauses to share his last sip of lemon-lime.

Crickets play music, inviting a dance,
While fireflies twinkle in a whimsical trance.
Every step is a skip, every corner a jest,
As critters unite for their nightly fest.

Beneath colorful blooms, where whimsy takes hold,
The joy of the garden is a pleasure untold.
With friends all around, and a pathway so bright,
Life unfurls beautifully, bursting with light.

www.ingramcontent.com/pod-product-compliance
Lightning Source LLC
Chambersburg PA
CBHW051643160426
43209CB00004B/768